D1565637

souvenirs of a shrunken world

for my grandparents,
who were there

selected by harryette mullen

2008 kore press first book award

souvenirs of a shrunken world

holly iglesias

Kore Press, Inc.
Tucson, Arizona USA
www.korepress.org

ISBN 13   978-1-888553-260
ISBN10   1-888553-26-X

Design by Lisa Bowden
Cover photographs © Valerie Galloway

All photographs inside the book are credited to the collections of the Missouri Historical Society, St. Louis. *(In the order in which they appear)* Geronimo. *Apache Chief from Arizona,* Official Photographic Company; *Taking of Bertillion Measurements,* measuring the height and reach of criminals; *Pygmy showing mutilated teeth* [Ota Benga, Pygmy from Belgian Congo], Jessie Tarbox Beals photographer; *Mrs. Wilkins teaching an Igorotte boy the cakewalk,* Jessie Tarbox Beals photographer.

contents

1. The new American 3

2. We wander from place to place 21

3. The bulk of the world's knowledge 35

4. The noblest lesson 49

5. American nervousness 61

6. You discover that romance 75

acknowledgments 88

notes 89

Running for the Fair, a Stereograph

Shaken from a dream about hoboes, a boy hightails it through the garden toward the tracks, his stride lengthening with the pace of escape—hen house, slop pot, ice box, cheese cloth—past and future neck and neck.

Air expanding with yeast in the kitchen, a girl cools her pulse at the pump and stares at the rhubarb, the peas, the sausage casings in a basin. She hears the train, bolts to watch it pass, cars strobing the corn fields into a picture show.

The new American, whether consciously or not, had turned his back on the nineteenth century before he was done with it.

—Henry Adams

1.

Façade

The park fills with noise, saws, hammers, gossip, complaints about the mud, flies, the cow gone dry. Glad for the work, the lot of us, camped in tents and abandoned streetcars. My Larry hangs plaster, huge gewgaws molded by the Italians, on the palaces taking shape behind falsework.

Baby's due any day, bigwigs planning a fuss. For the papers, not me. My job is to push her out, then present us proper for the baptism, quaint little family all cleaned up. Priests and dignitaries will press in for the photograph, their faces close to hers in hope of sharing the fame—Louisiana Purchase O'Leary, first-born of the Fair.

New Moon

A lamp inside my breast like a miner's, slashing darkness to find a seam, my ribs a cage for the beast inside pacing. Racing for the train, we are a cyclone of knickers and pinafores, nickels and gum drops.

Twelve, I am twelve, and I will act the lady. Take ice cream in a dish and touch door knobs only with my hanky. I will ride the Wheel, once, and no screaming.

They say that night is brighter than day at the Fair. That women swoon at the sights. But I shall keep my eyes open, watch the Igorots dance, shake hands with a Pygmy, knowing that he sings when he courts and when he kills. And if I see a girl half naked, her breast small and bronze as summer, will I reach out to cup it, as I do mine in dreams?

Emmaus House, Miss Harding Reporting

Our representatives patrol Union Station daily, ever on the lookout for girls who are strangers and alone. Promise of employment at the Fair is the standard ruse to lure them from small towns and even overseas, like the Germans who barely escaped being used for immoral purposes. Under my superintendency, we have sheltered nearly two hundred young women, not including the eight maids of Fair Japan who slipped away before even lighting upon their assigned cots, nor those already fallen unfortunates who are transported directly to the rescue home.

Flossie & T. R.

She lingers at Station No. 12 in a flirtatious hat and a cotton waist starched beyond comfort. *Sonnets from the Portuguese* on her lap, a prop for conversation, like the swan-head umbrella. Her assets are few—a talent for blushing and the convent education of little use to the beau awaiting her at the Tyrolean Alps for nearly an hour.

A carriage passes, a flash of light, the glare of a monocle, perhaps, or dazzling teeth. His gaze trains upon her, palpable as he tips his hat. The color rises in her face, spite banging in her breast as she refuses him a smile.

Foundling

Her mouth led her here, her milky mouth, her souring-in-the-sun mouth. And where will it all end with the Incubators closed for the day? Half faint, she had hoped to see the infants behind glass, the porcelain cases warmed to the temperature of a womb. To stand behind a velvet rope and guess which among them might be hers. Fifteen, tomorrow remote as the moon, she moves on, her shoe glancing against a soap-baby souvenir, dusty as a mulatto and just the size of her pocket.

Sashay

Lucy saunters up Targee Street, arms full of laundry, her gait scrutinized by a mother who still answers to Miz Fanny's Polly and old folk who suck their teeth at swishing skirts and coonjining swells, remembering all too well the price exacted for swagger. But Lucy is too busy to pay them any mind, conjuring visions of a ball at the Rosebud Café—cakewalk, sporting men, everybody ragging, then Joplin playing "The Cascades." The basket tumbles to the curb where Lucy leaves it, and heads to the drugstore, humming, for a soda.

New Century, New Woman, New St. Louis

Were it not for our dedication to municipal housekeeping, the World's Fair visitor might take home a memory of coal smoke and unpaved streets. Had we no concern for the loose class, tenements by the station might have remained rubbish piles. Had the Civic Improvement League simply busied itself with box suppers and quilting bees, the water might still be sludge, the color of a Morgan Street quadroon. Instead, we have launched an era of moral awakening.

Hygienics

A fouled pond of humanity, a standing menace, surely. Why just look at them, sleeping by the coal chute, a baby in the basket beneath the stairs. No privy, filthy sink, heaps of rags.

A bath house is needed.

An incinerator would do a world of good.

Dedication Group

They emanate from shallow space in grades of gray, Cleveland, Roosevelt, Francis. Arranged by height and heft, one balding, one hawk-beaked, the central figure rotund. He holds his top hat mid-chest, protecting his heart from the anarchist menace, perhaps. In the picture, the twentieth century is so new that their cutaways convey distinction, the striped pants and detachable collars not yet relegated to burlesque. Their eyes gaze in singular focus beyond the frame, as to a future unshadowed by Louisiana's purchase, which their well-pressed mass commemorates with gravity.

Sound of Wind and Limb

In the pink, we ran through the park before dawn, breasts bound, caps down tight, past barracks of sleeping acrobats and limp contortionists. At breakfast, our cheeks red as boys', we make a toast to Vigor with linden tea; and there the fun ends. We dress, a curse of starch and stays, finishing touches of gloves, parasols, hats, hers smart as her eyes, mine a flotilla of feathers.

Today is Agriculture—the Floral Clock, Missouri's corn dome, a suit made of binder twine, a pecan horse, the thirty-pound radish. And for last, refrigerated cases of sculptures in butter: the President, monocle and all, and the Discovery of St. Anthony Falls. We, mere painters of cufflinks and china cups, ponder the possibilities in a half-ton of dairy fat. Margaret says we could do better with chocolate. We'd require a studio, of course, and live models.

Swan Boat Gondolier

Embarking, they mouth soft words to the ladies—lagoon, woozy, wop—men with eight bits and an hour to kill. I am to sing as we float along, a quaint air to soothe the nerves of these princes of shoe leather and liver pills, these brewmeisters with old money stuffed into new pockets. They have paved their streets with the bones of our backs, scorned our saints and old-country hats. Walking home from our Saturday baths, we spit on the gates of their private streets, scowl through the grates at their children who are pale as dolls.

Neurasthenia, 1

In ten days, the nervous TROUBLE disappeared and the brain could think as hard and successfully as required. There's a reason for GRAPE-NUTS!

The NEW SCIENCE LIBRARY is a cure for mental paralysis. Learn what the famous Darwinian theory is; how the planets are weighed; what radium is. Send coupon for free specimen book.

A Message to Fleshy People from DOCTOR Henry C. Bradford of New York. No bandages or tight lacing or sickening pills, only my personal attention. Treatment for either SEX. Distance makes no difference. Satisfaction guaranteed.

Vagrant

May Harrington, Mary Cole, call her what you will. She's up to her old tricks whatever the name. Sergeant Dingle caught her at the Lindell Entrance and brought her in. Come along now, Mary, says he, we can't be loitering amongst the hoi poloi and traveling men now, can we?

All we can offer is soup and a cot for the night that's free of lice and debauch, more's the pity.

Weight 103. Height 5' 3-3/4". Head length 17.9. Fore arm, L., 41.8. Small mole just below L. wrist. Hair Dark Brown. Eyes Hazel. Complexion Sallow. Born 1874, Social Evil Hospital, St. Louis, Mo.

Third Visit

I took a flying trip through Manufactures to get the general idea. Exhibit of trunks, one water-proof like those used in the Japanese war. Scenes from the life of Christ, a pink diamond, the smallest watch in the world. Machine for making suspenders, display of very fine bath rooms. Took lunch with Emil and Blanche near Station No. 2. Concert by female quartet at the Missouri Building. At Foolish House, nearly laughed myself sick, then fire works at the grand basin before heading home.

I left considerable unseen.

Car fare .10   Admission .50   Soda .15   Intramural .10
Temple of Mirth .50   TOTAL 1.35

*We wander from place to place, not seeking to understand,
but yielding to the impressions waiting everywhere to woo us.*

—*World's Work,* August, 1904

2.

Margaret's Morning Constitutional on the Pike

Clowns and barkers. Dancing dogs the size of rats. A man in harem pants, a man in a serape and sombrero, a man scratching his fez. Daring Dan steadies himself, upside down on a tower of chairs, then slowly lifts his left hand. Ta-da! The feat robs her of breath, necessitating a stiff dose of Moxie before she can move along to the Statisticum.

Proof

It's a full day's journey from Cape Girardeau by wagon and train, but worth every minute for a chance to go round the world. To crawl in a Mexican mining gulch, stroll with Chippewas and Patagonians like we were neighbors and hear a real Philippine boy recite his tables. To survive the North Pole and muck through the sewers of Paris. To watch the Boer War or meet the timbermen of Hoo Hoo or touch a giant tortoise three hundred years old. Trust me, brother, I've done it all. Got the snapshots and postcards that say so.

Sizing Up

They circle round the meat spit and we circle round them, their bodies un-
abashed. We learn their names—Moro, Bontoc, Igorot, Negrito, Bagabo—
for they belong to us now. We need not fear them, their heads are shaped
like heads and some have hands the size of my own.

At home, Emma sing-songs at the table—*loin cloth, loin cloth*—until Papa
gets so rattled that he soaps her mouth.

Race for Space

A noisome lot, these immigrants washing ashore day after day. We do not know them, nor they us, but swiftly do we grow to resemble one another. Where will the sum of us ever fit?

The map is a picture of the soul, ours once vast and virginal, multitudes skittering across it like dice. Now, the frontier closed, what line must next be drawn for a man to face his savage self, and tame him?

Jefferson guessed it would take three centuries to fill the Purchase, yet lo! in a blink have we swarmed it. Teeming in towns and tenements, in trains and manufactories, are we to weave our dreams from the soot of a million smoke stacks, to sow liberty's seed in an open sewer?

Model Factory: Preaching in Pictures

A. Improving Their Lot.

1. How the girls are taught cooking. 2. How the children learn gardening. 3. How the girls go upstairs. 4. Lunch for twenty-five cents a week.

B. A Modern Forge.

1. Earnest industry of eleven thousand workers. 2. Arms raised, sinews stretched. 3. Flames leaping, not a moment to lose. 4. The hammers descend and sparks fly. 5. Pride in the intelligence of American workingmen.

C. A Remarkable Scene.

1. The doors swing open. 2. Four thousand men and women. 3. Like a hive of swarming bees. 4. The crowd separates. 5. Why America has been so successful.

Geography of the Americas

While the island has its share of mulattos and blue-black Negroes, the true Cuban is not swarthy. Rather, he is pink and romantic, and, unlike the Porto Rican, refined. One-quarter of the land is currently the property of Americans.

The alabastrine Argentinean is a man of style. Like us, he too is almost quit of the Indian problem, having cleared the pampas at last for the grazing of sheep. The Patagonian giant walks the road to extinction, and thus the Fairgoer is lucky to see him while he can.

Charitable Professions

Mister, I'm not one for namby-pamby reformers, but if you're looking for a faceful, you can't beat Social Economy. Even better, the missus will think you're getting uplifted, while left and right you'll see enough to put you in stitches. And no need to worry she'll join you; no sir, the ladies run out of there screaming at first sight of a tattoo or scabs or spit gobs in the saw-dust.

I liked the Tools of Thieves, myself, fingerprints, criminal histories and such. 'Course you got to barrel through a mountain of mollycoddle nonsense like a model prison cell and the class for lunatics and defectives, but at the end of the day, you'll be glad you went. Especially if you stop by the Battle Creek room and stick your feet in the vibrator.

Miss Roosevelt, Stopped in Her Tracks

The only urge she shares with the crowd is to leave some mark, some tiny scar on the log cabins, those relics of the great men of our brief past. She circles a primitive structure, upon its walls the mounted heads that serve as testament to her father's prowess in the wild. She finds the perfect spot, works her autograph in splendid little tacks.

A L I C E

The remainder of her day is dedicated to the Philippine Reservation, where a photographer stalking her captures the rare sight of her at a halt. She faces a Moro man, the muscles of his stomach clearly defined, a curious smile parting his lips. Alice, transfixed.

At the Close of the Day

There is a veil, dear, that drops as dusk creeps in like a truant. A witching hour, when we who have wiled away the afternoon among a million gay delights take pause. The sky melts from pink to mauve. The crowd quiets into a single accord. Only the Cascades speak, and we surrender to its language like converts desperate for redemption. Oh rarest of moments, oh mysterious shroud of night!

The Entertainers

Joplin admonishes the parlor pianist—*Slow down!*—while up and down Market Street clubs explode with players who define prowess in terms of speed. At the Rosebud Café, syncopators feed on gossip and cutting contests as they wait for messengers dispatched to hire them. Black and white alike may fear it, but ragtime's the rage, even if it does scramble the brain and corrupt youth.

Cooch Dancers

Princess Raj arches back, her spine lithe as a strop, until her head reaches the floor. Righting herself, the fringe of her bodice quivers as she begins to dance, the crowd gasping, their limbs knotted with desire. Backstage, Little Egypt waits for the lights to fade, veiled eyes laughing for love of the gentler sex.

Feria

We never go home, we stay and stay, in huts or barracks or plaster cliffs. But Sundays are ours, free of the obligation to pose for strangers. Fathers and mothers hover at the perimeter of the sandbox, humming in alien tongues, first head to head, then opening outward, gesticulating tales of their beautiful lands. Hammocks sway in the breezeway, empty until tomorrow, when the visitors' children will gladly sleep. We are too busy for rest, laughing in the shade of private languages, drawing intricate maps of our villages in the dust.

The bulk of the world's knowledge is an imaginary construction.

—Helen Keller

3.

Departed Darkness

How to shape a story or dance with the moon in a forest without night? Months now without tales of chameleons singing or nuts raining from the sky.

Confined to huts thatched with grasses long dead, we mourn the canopy that once sheltered and fed us. Outside, their ceaseless sun, a world without rest, the scent of fear on the wind.

Hats larger than hives pass by, the heads of their women erupting for want of magic.

The Graduate

In the exercise of judgment, into what errors are we liable to fall?
    Prejudice, an excited imagination, or ignorance.
Why does the appearance of an object differ from its facts?
    Because of its position and its distance from the observer.
Where are the emphatic positions in a sentence?
    At the end and at the beginning.
What is the general function of flowers?
    The development and perfection of seeds.
What is the distinguishing quality of hydrogen?
    It is the lightest substance known.
Are all the saints in Heaven equally happy?
    No.

Centennial: Against the Grain

In 1804, President Jefferson dispatched Lewis and Clark to find the North-west Passage, to chart a vast wilderness, to greet all tribal peoples with a message of good will. *Children, the Spaniards have surrendered. Hencefor-ward we become your fathers and friends. You shall have no cause to lament the change.*

Their return was met with wild celebration, of forests and rivers and animals beyond counting, of entire geographies reined in with compass and pen. In St. Louis, the men were greeted as though they had been to the moon.

Today, we see their trek as the seed of our manhood, the bittersweet pass-ing of youth. Thus it is fitting to honor them with a view to both past and future, judging progress against the measure of mercy, profit against pa-tience.

Geronimo, Tiger of the Human Race

I hear the Pygmy sing across the way day and night. Ota Benga, he scares the shadow-men with his tricks and the women with his pointed teeth. But to us, he's a man still free to roam.

The hunter buried inside me, I whittle toy bows and arrows, pose in a top hat like the One-Eyed Father in Washington who refuses to release me. When Ota sings his name to me, I cannot reply, having surrendered mine to strangers for twenty-five cents.

Zulu

Inside the kraal, an offering of feathers and spears, antlers and cook pots. Umkalali, an enormous tooth across his chest like a crescent moon, emerges from the hut to take his seat. Ankles crossed, hands folded, he is the regal center, men and boys in a fond cluster around him, some standing, some reclining on a carpet of leopard and tiger hides. A youth forgets to remove his thumb from his mouth; no one thinks to take down the string of lights before the flash explodes.

We Take Their Measure

The criminal skull displays a telltale bulge at the brow.

The syphilitic's gaze, like the cretin's, resembles that of the red squirrel.

Common pickpockets have thumbs ten percent smaller than average.

Slavic defectiveness manifests in their women as enlarged calves, as coarse hair in the men.

The Chinaman's propensity to laziness and chicanery is correlative to a liver several ounces shy of normal.

Transport of Igorot brains to the Smithsonian Institution for further study has been arranged by Dr. Hrdlicka.

A Romance of War and Its Simulation

One-armed Cronje cuts quite the figure as he takes his bride after a brief yet pious courtship. The general and the widow a study in contrasts, she demure in a plain gray gown, sweet peas tumbling from her arms; he somber in dress and expression, weary, perhaps, of the war. Of Boers charging the same hill over and over, horses writhing on the field as ambulances collect the wounded once again. Pondering which fate is worse: the hero's daily cycle of death and resurrection, or facing an army of Kodakers waiting for the couple to kiss.

Headliners

Fearless Midgets Of The Congo Valley. For The First Time They Will Set Foot On The Western Hemisphere. Some Queer Facts About Them.

Pygmies Discard Palm Leaf Suits For Warmer Clothing. Indian Neighbors Lend Them Blankets To Keep From Freezing.

Declare Americans Treat Them As They Would Monkeys. "They Laugh At Us And Poke Umbrellas Into Our Faces."

Driven From Huts By Rainstorm. Pygmies And Ainus Seek Shelter For Night In Indian School. Resembles Noah's Ark.

The Degenerate Classes

The unfit at present are coming to our shores in vast numbers as ethnic changes to our stock increase the likelihood of race annihilation. Philanthropic institutions are segregating the feeble-minded in order to prevent propagation.

The anarchist knows there is no better school to prepare men for revolution than that of poverty. In an open letter to the Unemployed, the Disinherited and the Miserable, one reads with alarm: *Learn the use of explosives.*

Model Student

We did our sums without fussing, recited the new pledge to the flag, and finished with a flourish of dumb-bell exercises. Now, beneath a willow, I await the reward, my first ice cream cone. Eyes half shut to the sights—Festival Hall, the Cascades tumbling toward a sea of bowlers and bonnets, gondolas drifting by—vision becomes a heavy cloud of slumber and contradiction. Snow on the Pike, summer everywhere else and no way to know if I'm dreaming.

Moment of Capture

The image reveals our accommodation, each detail flat as the misremembered past. A mocassined woman born in 1812, another dressed in calico and beads, men in feather crowns and neckties. A single boy wears suspenders. The words below say we Chippewa are *docile, industrious, clannish.*

Will Feigns a Fall

Champeen roper, that Kid, spiraling a lariat around him like a cyclone, talking all the while. Lanky and lean, he pleases the ladies, posing beside the pistol-packing cowboy statue, just smiling to beat the band. Sundays, he plays the Cummins Wild West Show in the Little Bighorn scene. The only quiet you'll ever hear on the Pike is when Custer and his men fall from their horses. But even that's broken when the Kid gets up, dusts himself off, grinning from ear to ear like his Cherokee blood didn't make a lick of difference.

The noblest lesson learned in life is self-control.

—on a blackboard in the Model School

4.

Model Child

The Navajo weaver on the floor has discovered me gazing at her child, the rest of the throng pressing forward, oblivious to the bundled papoose in the corner, quiet as a quilt. My own mother spares me a nickel a week from my wages and I have bought a Kodak, of which I am quite proud, but slip it slowly now, from my wrist to my bag, lest this woman one day remember me with dread.

Dimensions of Light

This bewitching statue captures not only the spirit of the electrical age but a new ideal of beauty as well. The model, Sylvia Starr, has caused quite a stir in DeVere's High Rollers and, in the process, created a more robust standard for the American girl. Five foot five, she is a splendid specimen of womanliness, one hundred and fifty pounds in perfect proportion—thirty-five, thirty-two, thirty-eight, the foot and leg measuring ten and thirty-five inches respectively. Do not fail to catch her in "Visions of Art."

Elementary Demonstrations

We dance and the camera captures us in motion. Behind us, the walls and desks and books look dead. Moments ago we were moving, and we will continue to move through a miracle unknown when we were born.

At the Philippine school, they sit. They read and raise their hands. Because they are un-learning, there is no dancing, just haircuts and long pants and primers. I watch Antero, who is twelve, like me. He knows English, but I want him to speak Tagalog, language of the river.

The Bookkeeper Flirts with Danger

Serpentine shot through the air like meteors, confetti rained in torrents upon a thousand pedestrians. Din of cowbells and whistles and megaphones. Every hat was a target for the inflated bladder, no respect for age or dignity. Oh, how I wanted to be a boy again, be a little bad!

If the Pike were a mile longer, it would lead to hell.

Drawing from Life

Sight trained to a reduced scale, I sketch on notecards, exercise patience in expectation of the numinous detail. All along the lagoon, easelists try in vain to cram the mammoth palaces into a frame, to halt the passing throng in service to Art. But work that fits a pocket suits me best—a blistered toe, candy corn, the cubbyholes at Lost and Found.

Today, a single brass button on the cuff of a soldier who pierces the vast oceans of the world with pins, each one marking the position of a battleship on the map inside Government.

Pilar Ponders the Pecking Order

Now it is English to learn, English to teach—to savages, *por Dios*. I wear the long white gown, I speak five languages, my hair is rolled in the European style, I am a lady, a Christian, a professor from Manila who teaches teachers, the best, not packs of wild primitives.

The U. S. government displays me teaching Bagabo, Igorot and Moro children in a thatched shack. I, a woman in a white gown, educated by nuns, refined, light-skinned, a Zamora. We do not mix with these people. They are riddled with disease and superstition. They live in huts on the Fairgrounds. Would the Americans have me sleep with them, too?

American Impressionists

A sleeve of her waist dangles from the chair where she tossed it. Cotton lawn, white on white, a hint of shade and motion. A stove the color of patience, the single plane of my bed, desire interrupted by the glare of morning.

Clothed, we resume solidity and leave for the Palace of Fine Arts. Observe, if you will, how the French parse light, sever form from contour and release it into constellations. See how fragments flicker and fade like faces on the Pike. Electricity as foil to Nature, lovers embracing in shadow.

Miniatures

I roamed the grounds for days like an Arab in the desert, searching for something just right for my wife, stuffing my pockets with buttons, pins, calendars you could lose in a breeze, till I tossed them in the rubbish. Each trinket felt smaller than experience, too cheap for the weight of our time apart or the cruel quiet of her confinement. Twelfth birth in ten years and who can say if the tiny soul will make it to winter, or when she might allow him a name. I would heap the mantel with souvenirs of a shrunken world to amuse her—gunboats, telephones, geisha girls, canoes—but I fear she is beyond diversion. My present hope fits in my hand, a silver-plate walnut with a clasp, inside a fan of vistas reduced to a bearable size.

Man Made of Facts

He avoids the Main Picture, the enormous fan of palaces that draws thousands into its folds. Each building larger than life, than a million lives, how to enter the first conundrum. A serious man, a man of purpose, he finds the Pike charmless. He comes to learn, to be uplifted, to improve his powers of observation. From the deck of the Wireless Tower, he peers in all directions, jotting on a small pad. He washes down the calculations with a root beer at dusk, then scurries for the streetcar. How he hates the evening crowds, the predictable oohs and ahs when the illuminations begin.

American nervousness is the product of American civilization.

—George M. Beard

5.

Sister,

I fear that we may lose him. He hangs by a thread, mumbling and fitful. He refuses beef tea, porridge, even the slice of toasted bread. He collapsed by the Temple of Mirth and a guard brought him home, carried him into the parlor actually, a rather tall fellow with gold braid on his shoulders. Well, yes, collapsed, I tell you, a bag of peanuts in his hand, and no hat. And goodness knows his nerves are shot, business being what it is and he suffering from coffee heart.

What will I tell mother? The Fair has taken its toll and who's to blame? A man such as he has no place in that wild bamboozle of harem girls and hucksters and diving horses. Please, dear, be quick. Finish with the beans and squash, of course, but oh! do come soon.

St. Louis Provident Association: Applications for Relief

1. German woman, quite dirty and deaf, speaks little English. Husband a musician who sent to Iowa for her and three sons after finding work. Upon arrival, she found him departed to Memphis leaving no word or funds. Asking for shelter and food.

2. Spaniard with a French wife and three children. Scheme was to exhibit a sea lion from Havana at the fair, but said creature died in transport. After stuffing, unable to sell it as a specimen. Room rent in arrears. Request for transportation to New Orleans for self and family.

3. Single man, 24, former clerk in Kentucky. Writes a good hand, fairly educated. Failed to find employment, though receiving board for dishwashing. Wishes to be transported back home.

Railroad and Transportation Day

Though the grounds are wild with parades, miles of wagons and floats, water launches, automobiles, miniature trains, I came for the men on foot. Mechanics marching in formation, three city blocks of white uniforms moving in a single mass, a flit of the eye the only distinction between comrade and foe.

Nervous, some of them search the sea of faces for old strikers, those of us who still honor the blood of the slain with emblems of a brief triumph, small defiances among the over-heated crowd—mine a blue cap torn from the head of a scab.

Change of Venue

In a blink, we moved to the church and withdrew from the roster of congresses at the Fair. We are righteous, we have work to do. No time to cry over Negro Day, which was nothing but a sop in the first place.

On the agenda: Miss Bowen on her success with Anti-Hair-Wrapping Clubs, a report from Sumner High's Twentieth Century Girls Club, and a discussion on the damage done by coon songs.

Long let us remember the words of our president, Annie Jones, who cleverly used the statistics of the dominant race to inspire us: *The fact that we pay taxes on $460,000,000 worth of property would seem to indicate that we can at last show clear title to something other than mansions in the skies.*

Up to Their Old Tricks

Seventy-five thousand people pack into the Plaza St. Louis on the hottest day of the year for the Pygmy dance. The savages, half naked, brandish spears and knives in a well-practiced imitation of tribal rituals, the audience thrilling to the simulation of violence. Indulging an antic impulse, the dancers charge to the edge of the stage, crossing an invisible line as titillation dissolves into panic. Blood curdling war cries are countered by shrieks from women as the crowd heaves instinctively forward. An entire regiment is required to restore order. The Africans, escorted back to their huts, set up a chatter through the night that sets the nerves on edge.

Civilizing Impulse

A Wichita woman drives a stake into the ground beside her grass lodge. Upon it she nails a placard: *No Photos.* In the Igorot Village a sign on hut No. 9: *Visitors Strictly Forbidden to Enter This House.*

•

The Ainu elder leads his family in a ritual to honor ancestors and implore their protection. His fingers stroke the inau, a carved offering-stick brought from home, they the first of their people ever to leave the island. Later he hides it for fear someone will steal it, these people so rude they press against the dwelling's single window, even during prayer.

•

Kwakiutl Indians request a fence be built around their campsite to protect their totem poles and store of baskets. They implore assistance in dealing with spectators and their *taking qualities.*

67

Maria Antonia Montoya Martinez, San Ildefonso Pueblo

My hands, Julian's hands shape something new from the old, a mystery of doubles and shadows, inside and out, black on black. Collectors come to the Cliff Dwellers exhibit to lift the jugs, to test the heft of possession, to calm themselves after exposing the frail bones of their feet in an X-ray machine.

We feign ignorance of English, releasing them to babble freely. I speak only Tewa in the presence of those who call us a dying breed, who dress our men as Hopi for the snake dance, these tourists lost in a land they call home.

Going the Distance

Dust and heat took their toll as Hicks ran the marathon, his doctors sponging him down, proffering the occasional tonic of brandy and strychnine along the way. Here we witnessed the first Olympian efforts on American soil, our man a product forged of gumption and science who performed like a well-oiled machine until hallucinations set in and he wandered off course.

Helen Keller Day

Some days I feel like a music box with the play shut up inside. Or a cloud in which one man sees his dream, another his nightmare. Surely we are all projections of one sort or another, and so the crowd grabs at me, tries to touch what delights and terrifies. Believing me an angel, they charge from all sides, tear my coat, rip a rose from my lapel, oblivious of my will, my impatient fingers, the senses yet named.

Datto Bulon's Vision

She descends from the tree hut in a swarm of keepers. Again on the ground they surround her, steering her past Antonio, typewriter on his lap. A ghost, her suit the color of doves and seashells, her face a pool of summer rain. Into her palm, a dark-haired woman presses her fingers. They laugh. Negotiations are made.

She knows I watch her, nostrils wide, chin held high. I stand perfectly still as she approaches. My hair, oiled and swept over one shoulder, welcomes the comb of her hands, her eyes, like bees, singing.

Julia Davis and the Reconstruction of Heaven

We take our rightful seats on the Wheel for the world's greatest ride. We, grandchildren of slaves, we the prize and the promise, the lifting of the veil.

Hundreds and hundreds of humans joined in a circuit of perfect joy and bewilderment. Men in turbans, men in homburgs, dowagers in mourning weeds, sweethearts, strangers, enemies, all released from gravity.

We pause to take on more passengers, the car rocking like a cradle. Across the way, Geronimo's face against the glass, eyes wide to take in the whole valley with a single glance.

And When I Die

You will mourn me beyond the fact of this body. Whether it froze in a box car or starved for want of native food, time was lost to me the moment we arrived at this place. I vacated my skin, freed my soul to simply watch as is the custom here, to endure the harvest dance without crops, the wedding bridge trampled by boys who do as they please.

My prayer for you is one of time restored to natural order, my fear that our hearts will be taken to their capital in jars.

*You discover that romance has a history
and lo! romance has vanished.*

—Jack London

6.

Testimonial

Lily Langtry's endorsement and a desire to preserve my complexion sufficed to induce a visit to the Bubble Fountain, where I was delighted to sample Fairy Soap. Little did I anticipate, however, the entertaining antics of the Gold Dust Twins, adorable darkies who keep the crowd in stitches, juggling platters and washing clothes in a mountain of suds. A considerable improvement over their predecessors, I understand, a less tractable duo who played craps and indulged in fisticuffs the livelong day. Well, all I can say is that I came for my skin and left laughing! You can bet I'll let Gold Dust Washing Powder do my work for me from now on.

Manual Education

The Palace of Machinery teems with processes and products alike—electric potato mashers, turbines, typewriters, batteries—though what haunts me is the image of blind boys making brooms, their exquisite fingers tamping straw, chins raised in expectation, one so intense his thoughts are nearly visible as I place myself in the path of his gaze, steeled for the thrill of it passing through me like an X-ray.

We Know the Mothers

Would find us frivolous, wasting the hard-to-come-by dollar on a roller chair
while they boil sheets in the tenement yard. Grateful, of course, that we've
hauled the kids off for the day, but oblivious to the rigors particular to the
Fair. Energy sapped by noon, we deposited the toddlers at the playground,
left the older ones at Liberal Arts, where they are duty-bound to await our
return, resolved as Miss Ernst and I are to visit the Swedenborgians and
Social Economy, for professional uplift. The collegian driving the chair flirts
into the crown of our hats, too full of himself to notice our exhaustion, or the
way I hook her pinkie with mine as we pass the East Lagoon.

Neurasthenia, 2

Does Your Head Contain a Story? The human BRAIN is a money mine. If yours is not paying properly, why not develop it by digging some clever idea out of it? THE BLACK CAT, your Stepping Stone to Success. Five cents.

The main cause of unhappiness, ill-health, sickly children and divorce is ignorance of the laws of self and sex. Learn the truth in SEXOLOGY ILLUS-TRATED. Write for Free Table of Contents. Puritan Publishing Co., Dept. A, Philadelphia.

Are Your Legs STRAIGHT? If not, wear our Pneumatic and Cushion-Rubber Forms. Illustrated pamphlet mailed under plain letter seal.

When the NERVES need food, pure beer is the usual prescription. The doctor knows that it's good for you because malt and hops feed the nerves. That is why the doctor says, "SCHLITZ."

Anthropometry

Four prints, artless and sheer as ash. The soles of two pairs of Ainu feet—Yazo, Shirake—the palm of an Ainu hand—Shutratek—and the footprint of a Bagabo—unnamed—demonstrating the effects of several weeks of shoe-wearing.

Ethnologists call the Ainu "people of the single idea" because they think only one thought at a time.

Beyond Her Years

When I am of an age, I shall beg to be questioned and happily tell. I will say that memory is grander than any vista carved from raw prairie, that I first recognized myself at the Fair in a sea of faces, in flickering images that linger to this day. I will show trinkets and postcards, the only proof. Mere children, we learned more in a week than we could forget in a lifetime, our wildest dreams surpassed, our minds still puzzled by the splendors of a transitory paradise.

One of the Happiest Days of Our Quiet Lives

We had our day, same as the President, I figure, though I would like to have had my Thanksgiving supper with kids from around the world. They have their own languages and wouldn't care if we didn't talk. The papers say there were presents and flowers and cake for everyone. We boys from the Home wanted to stay for the fireworks, but the girls were much relieved to go beforehand, scared the explosion might make vibrations in their stomachs.

Stroke of Midnight

President Francis addresses the crowd, then pushes a lever that plunges the Fairgrounds into darkness. Fireworks the only light,

F A R E   W E L L   G O O D   N I G H T

voices tremulous as they rise from the departing throng: *We'll drink a cup of kindness yet for auld lang syne.*

Conversion Experience

To the Chicago House Wrecking Company goes the contract for demolition. The iron fence will remain in place during restoration of the park, palaces in the Main Picture to be razed within three months of the Fair's closing. Admission will be charged to view the wreckage.

The Iowa Building has been purchased for removal to its namesake state for use as an asylum for inebriates. The Temple of Fraternity will be converted into a consumptive sanitarium in New Mexico.

Dynamite detonates along girders of the Ferris Wheel. It shudders, crumples, sinks slowly to the earth. A boy tells the reporter it's like watching the execution of an old friend.

Too Long at the Fair

My Dear Husband,

     I hope your leg is all right.
     This afternoon we went to the Fair Grounds—ruin, desolation, not a stone left or the least sign. The lagoons are nothing but a rocky waste.
     I am home-sick for the Fair, and just as tired as if I had been there.

                        Your affectionate wife,

In the Dream an Electric Fan

Soothes me—past heat, into sleep, the whir entering my ears, my grand-
child's ears, quiet as the future. We meet at a crossroads, recognize one
another by our buttons and pins. She weeps for want of all I know, unaware
that our memory lies buried inside her: mother's abandoned village, an Ad-
vent hymn, the recipe for pineapple cake I rushed to copy at Agriculture,
frantic that I'd miss the train, yelling to Emma, *Wait for me, wait!*

Attempting the Impossible

1.
Words fail.
The scale immense, distances enormous.

2.
Addicted to the use of superlatives, the mind reels.

3.
A revelation, its beauty indescribable.

4.
At a loss what to do.
Who wants to think of going home? Home is a fool.

5.
Reconciled to the end of the Fair.
Passed into history, vanished like a thing of air.

6.
It cannot even be hinted at by words.

acknowledgments

"Sister," "Hygienics," and "Flossie & TR," appeared in *Margie Review,* Vol. 2, 2003, in slightly different form.

"Margaret's Morning Constitutional on the Pike," "Beyond Her Years," "Third Visit," "Sizing Up," "Attempting the Impossible," "Charitable Professions," "Proof," "Change of Venue," "Model Factory: Preaching in Pictures," and "Miniatures" appeared in *Gateway,* Vol. 24, No. 4, Spring 2004.

notes

see website for complete notes on the text: www.korepress.org

for section dividers:

page 2   Henry Adams, *Autobiography of Henry Adams* (1907)

page 20   *World's Work* magazine (1904)

page 34   Helen Keller, *The World I Live In* (1908)

page 48   written on the blackboard in a photo of "A Model Classroom" exhibit

page 60   George M. Beard, *American Nervousness, Its Causes and Consequences* (1881)

page 74   Jack London, *The Kempton-Wace Letters* (1903)

for poems:

"Neurasthenia, 1." Sources: *The Cosmopolitan,* September, 1904, and *World's Work,* August, 1904.

"Third Visit." Source: *Diary of Edmund Philibert.* Philibert's diary, along with those of Edward V.P. Schneiderhahn and Sam P. Hyde and the correspondence of Florence Philibert McCallion (Philibert's sister) are archived at the Missouri Historical Society in St. Louis. Portions of these materials were published in *Indescribably Grand: Diaries and Letters from the 1904 World's Fair,* edited and with an introduction by Martha R. Clevenger (1996).

"Model Factory: Preaching in Pictures." Source: Photo captions, *The Cosmopolitan,* September, 1904.

"The Graduate." Source: Senior examination book of Florence Gay, 1903, possession of the author.

"Headliners." Source: National and local press coverage of Pygmies at the Fair, reprinted in *Ota: the Pygmy at the Zoo*, by Phillips Verner Bradford and Harvey Blume (1992).

"The Degenerate Classes." Source: Robert Hunter, *Poverty* (1904).

"The Bookkeeper Flirts with Danger." Source: Diary of Sam P. Hyde.

"St. Louis Provident Association: Applications for Relief." Source: *Charities,* Oct. 8, 1904.

"Neurasthenia, 2." Sources: *The Cosmopolitan,* September, 1904 and *World's Work,* August, 1904.

"Too Long at the Fair." Source: Correspondence of Florence Philibert McCallion.

"Attempting the Impossible." Sources: Diaries of Edward V. P. Schneiderhahn and Sam P. Hyde.

the author

Holly Iglesias is a poet, editor and translator. Her publications include *Hands-On Saints,* a chapbook of poems, and *Boxing Inside the Box: Women's Prose Poetry,* a work of literary criticism. She teaches in the Master of Liberal Arts Program at the University of North Carolina-Asheville.

Author photograph by Catherine Reid.

kore press

We express our deep gratitude to those who helped make the Kore Press First Book Award possible: The Tucson-Pima Arts Council, The Arizona Commission on the Arts, through appropriations from the Arizona State Legislature and the National Endowment for the Arts, the manuscript readers, the judge, and all the writers who submitted their work.

Previous first book award winners: Jennifer Barber for *Rigging the Wind,* selected by Jane Miller; Deborah Fries for *Various Modes of Departure,* selected by Carolyn Forché; Elline Lipkin for *The Errant Thread,* selected by Eavan Boland; Sandra Lim for *Loveliest Grotesque,* selected by Marilyn Chin; and Spring Ulmer for *Benjamin's Spectacles*, selected by Sonia Sanchez.

92